McPherson Goes to Church

D0731137

McPherson Goes to Church

John McPherson

ZondervanPublishingHouse

Grand Rapids, Michigan

A Division of HarperCollinsPublishers

McPherson Goes to Church
copyright © 1994 John McPherson

Requests for information should be addressed to:
Zondervan Publishing House
Grand Rapids, MI 49530

McPherson, John, 1959–
    McPherson goes to church / by John McPherson.
      p.   cm.
    ISBN 0-310-48181-3 (softcover)
    1. Church attendance—Caricatures and cartoons. 2. American wit and humor, Pictorial. I. Title.
    NC1429.M476A4   1994
    741.5'973—dc20   94–31457
                                            CIP

All rights reserved. No part of this publication may be reproduced, stored in a retrieval system, or transmitted in any form or by any mean—electronic, mechanical, photocopy, recording, or any other —except for brief quotations in printed reviews, without the prior permission of the publisher.

Cover design by Chris Gannon

Printed in the United States of America

94 95 96 97 98 99 00 01 02 03 / CH / 10 9 8 7 6 5 4 3 2 1

"THIS NEW CHOIR DIRECTOR CERTAINLY HAS SPUNK!"

"REMIND ME NEVER TO ASK THE YOUTH GROUP TO HELP FOLD THE CHURCH BULLETINS AGAIN."

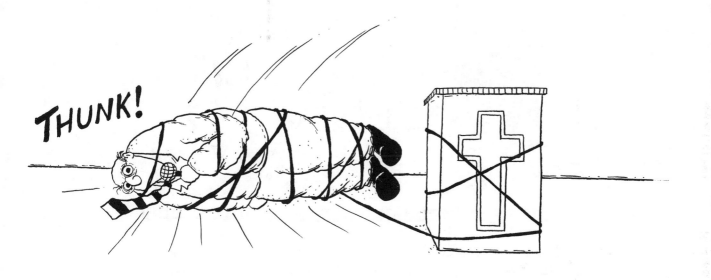

THIS INCIDENT PRETTY MUCH CONVINCED THE CONGREGATION TO PITCH IN AND GET PASTOR MENLEY A CORDLESS MICROPHONE.

"IT'S AN EXACT REPLICA OF GIANTS' STADIUM. WE'RE HOPING IT WILL ENTICE MORE HUSBANDS TO ATTEND."

THIS PARTICULAR PASTORAL SELECTION COMMITTEE WAS KNOWN FOR ITS THOROUGNESS.

"YOU BETTER DO AS THE SIGN SAYS. PASTOR SPIFFNER'S SERMONS TEND TO BE A BIT ON THE LIVELY SIDE."

"OUR DONATIONS HAVE DOUBLED SINCE WE HAD THAT THING INSTALLED!"

THE PARSONAGE COMMITTEE WAS STUNNED WHEN, FOR THE FIRST TIME IN CHURCH HISTORY A NEW PASTOR AND HIS WIFE THOUGHT THE PARSONAGE WAS GREAT THE WAY IT WAS.

"I THINK IT'S ABOUT TIME SOMEBODY TOLD MRS. NURLSPAR WE DON'T ACCEPT DEPOSIT SODA CANS FOR THE OFFERTORY."

"BOBBY HERE IS HELPING OUT UNTIL THE BELL GETS BACK FROM THE REPAIR SHOP."

THE GLENVIEW CHURCH SEARCH COMMITTEE HAD A KNACK FOR COMING UP WITH REALLY ANNOYING INTERVIEW QUESTIONS.

"I'M HOPING THESE NEW SPEAKERS WILL GIVE MY SERMONS A LITTLE MORE PUNCH."

THE BANFORD VALLEY CHURCH STOOPS TO RAW COMMERCIALISM IN ITS ATTEMPT TO INCREASE ATTENDANCE.

"FOR PETE'S SAKE, I'VE BEEN HERE FOR TWELVE YEARS! WILL YOU PLEASE STOP REFERRING TO ME AS 'THE NEW PASTOR'!"

BUDGET PODIUM.

"PERSONALLY, I THINK THIS DONATION THING IS GETTING OUT OF HAND."

CLEARLY, THE NEW ORGANIST WAS NOT GOING TO WORK OUT.

INUNDATED WITH REQUESTS FOR COUNSELING, PASTOR MARTIN LEMPLER REALIZED IT WAS TIME HE STARTED SCREENING PEOPLE BEFORE GIVING THEM A SLOT ON HIS SCHEDULE.

"NEXT TIME WE HAVE THE PEWS REFINISHED, LET'S REMEMBER TO HAVE IT DONE ON A MONDAY, NOT A SATURDAY."

SCANDAL ROCKED THE MAPLE VALLEY CHURCH WHEN IT WAS DISCOVERED THAT THE CHOIR HAD BEEN LIP-SYNCING FOR THE LAST SIX YEARS.

THE MILTON SPRINGS CHURCH WAS DESPERATELY IN NEED OF A MASTER PLAN.

"SINCE TODAY'S SERVICE IS BEING TAPED FOR COMMEMORATIVE PURPOSES, WE ASK THAT THE FOLLOWING INDIVIDUALS PLEASE REFRAIN FROM SINGING DURING THE HYMNS: ALICE ZUTMAN, ED FROMP, CAROL VIDMAR,..."

MANY FELT THAT PASTOR NORTLEY'S OBSESSION WITH FITNESS WAS BEGINNING TO INTERFERE WITH HIS WORK.

NEW PASTOR RALPH MUMFORD HAD HIS WORK CUT OUT FOR HIM.

BY AWARDING MEDALS TO ANYONE WHO SERVES ON A
COMMITTEE, THE WINSLOW PRESBYTERIAN CHURCH DRAMATICALLY
INCREASED THE CONGREGATION'S VOLUNTEERISM.

MRS. McGURTY PRIDED HERSELF IN BEING ABLE TO HIT THE COLLECTION PLATE FROM THE BALCONY.

PASTOR DAVE SLODMAN INDULGES IN ONE OF HIS FAVORITE DAYDREAMS.

CHANGING THAT PESKY LIGHT IN THE SANCTUARY REQUIRED A TEAM EFFORT BY MEMBERS OF THE CONGREGATION.

"THE REST OF THE BELL CHOIR IS OUT WITH THE FLU."

DUE TO A SCHEDULING ERROR, THE LADIES' QUILTING CLUB AND THE YOUTH BASKETBALL LEAGUE WERE HELD SIMULTANEOUSLY IN THE CHURCH GYMNASIUM.

PASTOR DAVE CALHOON WAS TRYING DESPERATELY TO MAKE HIS SERMONS MORE LIVELY.

ATTENDANCE INCREASED BY 60 PERCENT AFTER THE RECLINERS WERE INSTALLED.

STU DAWSON FOUND THAT OFFERING A LITTLE INCENTIVE GREATLY INCREASED THE ENTHUSIASM FOR THE FAMILY'S NIGHTLY DEVOTIONS.

PASTOR LIMKIN WAS EXTREMELY DISAPPOINTED WHEN HE DISCOVERED THAT THE CONGREGATION'S SHOW OF TOGETHERNESS WAS ACTUALLY CAUSED BY A BROKEN FURNACE.

REVEREND NORDSTROM FINALLY FOUND AN EFFECTIVE WAY TO RESOLVE CHURCH CONFL'CTS.

"DIRECT THE YOUTH CHOIR? UH... SURE, NO PROBLEM. WHAT? NO, GLAD TO DO IT! REALLY."

NEWCOMERS TO *TWINDLE VALLEY CHURCH* QUICKLY SENSED THAT THIS WAS A CONGREGATION WITH TWO VERY DISTINCT FACTIONS.

"AND NOW A FEW WORDS FROM LOIS FARNSLEY, WHO IS LOOKING FOR SOME VOLUNTEERS TO HELP OUT WITH THE FOUR-TO-SIX-YEAR-OLD SUNDAY SCHOOL CLASS."

UPON VISITING HIS FORMER CHURCH JUST THREE MONTHS AFTER LEAVING, PASTOR BRUCE FERNLOCK DISCOVERS THAT HIS IMPACT THERE WASN'T NEARLY AS PROFOUND AS HE HAD THOUGHT.

"I THINK WE NEED TO HAVE A TALK WITH THE ALTAR BOY."

THE PASTORAL SELECTION COMMITTEE AT RUMSON VALLEY CHURCH WAS LOUSY AT MAKING DECISIONS.

THUS FAR, THE MEMBERSHIP DRIVE FOR THE FELLOWSHIP COMMITTEE HAD BEEN VERY SUCCESSFUL.

PASTOR WAYNE KLEMPER DIDN'T RESPOND
WELL TO CRITICISM.

DUE TO THE GREETING PROCESS AT POTTER CREEK CHURCH, FIRST-TIME VISITORS RARELY BECAME SECOND-TIME VISITORS.

"I THINK IT'S TIME WE ALL PITCHED IN AND BOUGHT THE CHOIR SOME CLASSIER-LOOKING ROBES."

"THE ORGANIST CALLED IN SICK SO I HAD TO GET A LAST MINUTE REPLACEMENT."

McPHERSON

REVEREND SPILLMAN'S IDEA OF COMMUNITY INVOLVEMENT WAS VASTLY DIFFERENT FROM THAT OF THE CHURCH BOARD.

"I'D LIKE TO THANK ALL OF YOU FOR COMING THROUGH IN THE CLUTCH TO MAKE THIS YEAR'S CLOTHING DRIVE A BIG SUCCESS."

CLEARLY, PASTOR BORKMAN WAS GETTING DESPERATE
IN HIS ATTEMPTS TO FIND FRESH, NEW SERMON TOPICS.

PROPOSED NEW
PASTOR

McPHERSON

AN ARTIST'S CONCEPTION OF THE IDEAL
PASTORAL CANDIDATE BASED UPON INPUT FROM
THE SEARCH COMMITTEE.

"I'D LIKE TO OFFER MY APOLOGIES TO THOSE OF YOU WHO DIDN'T REALIZE THAT OUR VOLUNTEERS WERE SEALING THE PARKING LOT THIS WEEKEND."

SOME PEOPLE SAID THE CRIES OF JOY FROM THE SUNDAY SCHOOL TEACHERS COULD BE HEARD FROM MORE THAN A MILE AWAY.

CHILDREN'S CHOIR DIRECTOR RUTH LANG WATCHED TWO MONTHS OF PREPARATION FOR THE CHRISTMAS SERVICE GO DOWN THE TUBES, THANKS TO A BAG OF BUBBLE GUM.

STRICKEN BY A SUDDEN SPELL OF LARYNGITIS,
PASTOR FEGMAN SWITCHES ON THE AUTO-PASTOR.

"JANITOR? NO! THAT'S OUR ASSOCIATE PASTOR."

WHEN CHOIR DIRECTORS DREAM.

"IT'S CALLED CHURCH INVADERS! THE OBJECT IS TO GET YOUR PASTOR OUT OF THE CHURCH BEFORE HE GETS OVERRUN BY BOARD MEMBERS, WHO YOU CAN STUN WITH YOUR LASER IF THEY GET TOO CLOSE!"

ATTEMPTS TO MAKE THE CHURCH NEWSLETTER
MORE EXCITING TO READ WERE GETTING OUT OF HAND.

PASTOR LOU MUTNER BEGINS TO QUESTION HIS ROLE WITH THE BOARD.

THOUGH HE HAD RETIRED FROM THE CHURCH MORE
THAN THREE MONTHS AGO, FORMER PASTOR WALT LUTSKI
WAS FINDING IT HARD TO LET GO.

AS THE NEW PASTOR CONTINUED HIS SERMON, AN ANGRY MOB SEARCHED FOR MEMBERS OF THE PASTORAL SELECTION COMMITTEE.

"THEN IT'S SETTLED! WE PAINT THE SUNDAY SCHOOL ROOM BLUE!"

ALTHOUGH HE HAD PREACHED AT MANY RURAL CHURCHES, THE CONGREGATION AT ELK VALLEY CHURCH PRESENTED PASTOR WALT STIMPSON WITH A UNIQUE CHALLENGE.

PASTOR LOU BARNSLEY TRIES TO WIN BACK MEMBERS
THAT HE HAD LOST TO TV PREACHERS.

THE SEARCH COMMITTEE RETURNS FROM A
SUCCESSFUL OUTING.

"I THINK IT'S ABOUT TIME THEY BROKE DOWN AND GOT US SOME MICROPHONES."

YET ANOTHER PASTOR'S KID IS SADDLED WITH THE BURDEN OF HAVING TO LEAD A PERFECT LIFE.

PASTOR RALPH LUMBAR HAD SUBTLE WAYS OF REMINDING THE ASSOCIATE PASTORS OF THEIR SECOND-CLASS STATUS.

PASTOR WAGMAN KNEW HE WAS ON A ROLL WHEN THE
CONGREGATION STARTED DOING THE WAVE.

"I'D LIKE TO KNOW WHOSE BRIGHT IDEA IT WAS TO INSTALL EXTRA-PLUSH CARPETING IN THE SANCTUARY."

UNABLE TO AFFORD BELLS FOR A BELL CHOIR, MEMBERS OF THE ROCKY VALLEY CHURCH IMPROVISED AS BEST THEY COULD.

WITH THE HELP OF SLIDES FROM THE ANNUAL CHURCH PICNIC, PASTOR DALBY WAS ABLE TO RECRUIT SEVERAL NEW VOLUNTEERS.

PASTOR BURNBAUM HAD ENDURED SNORING DURING HIS SERMONS
IN THE PAST, BUT NEVER FROM HIS OWN WIFE.

"WHEN THEY TOLD US THEY WERE GOING TO EXPAND THE SANCTUARY, THIS WASN'T WHAT I HAD IN MIND."

PASTOR ALAN MILGRANE WAS DIRECTLY RESPONSIBLE FOR THE CHURCH'S DECISION TO ESTABLISH A DRESS CODE FOR PASTORS.

THE LATEST IN THE EVER-EXPANDING ARRAY OF CHRISTIAN PRODUCTS.

THAT HUMILIATING MOMENT WHEN YOU REALIZE THAT THE PROGRAM SAID TO SING VERSES ONE, TWO, AND THREE, BUT NOT FOUR.

THE WAGNERS STRUCK UPON A SURE-FIRE WAY TO GET THE NEIGHBORS TOGETHER FOR AN HOUR OF BIBLE STUDY.

A RARE TREAT FOR THE SINGLE PASTOR: BEING INVITED TO DINNER AND DISCOVERING IT'S _NOT_ A SET-UP FOR A BLIND DATE.

"LOOK, STAN, I'M SORRY ABOUT YOUR CAR. BUT, FRANKLY, I'M APPALLED THAT YOU, BEING A PASTOR, WOULD ALLOW YOURSELF TO BECOME UPSET OVER SOMETHING LIKE THIS.

NEW MEMBERS AT THE SANDY HILL CHURCH WERE OFTEN
OVERWHELMED BY THE INTENSE PRESSURE TO GET INVOLVED.

"TODAY'S COLLECTION WILL GO TOWARD THE PURCHASE OF A NEW ROOF."

CHOIR DIRECTOR RALPH STIMSON FACES THE FATEFUL TASK OF HAVING TO TELL THE NEW PASTOR'S WIFE THAT SHE HAS THE SINGING ABILITY OF AN AILING WATER BUFFALO.

THE HOTTER THE WEATHER BECAME, THE LESS PEOPLE
LIKED THE NEW NAUGAHYDE PEW CUSHIONS.

AT ABOUT 12:35 THE CONGREGATION STARTED TO DROP SOME SUBTLE HINTS THAT THE SERVICE WAS RUNNING TOO LONG.

THERE WERE THOSE IN THE CONGREGATION WHO FELT THAT YOUTH PASTOR STAN LEPLEY WENT TOO FAR IN TRYING TO APPEAL TO THE CHURCH'S TEENAGERS.

"MANY THANKS TO THE LADIES' QUILTING CLUB FOR PROVIDING US WITH THESE LOVELY NEW CHOIR ROBES."

THE CONGREGATION BEGAN TO DROP SOME SUBTLE HINTS THAT IT WAS TIME TO GET SOME PEW CUSHIONS.

"WARREN ZEFFEL WILL NOW GIVE US AN UPDATE ON THE ONGOING PROJECT TO GET RID OF THE BATS IN THE SANCTUARY."

WITH HIS COUNSELING SCHEDULE OVERFLOWING, PASTOR LARRY WERTZ WAS FORCED TO SEE NEW CASES AT EVERY AVAILABLE OPPORTUNITY.

THE WINSLOW BAPTIST CHURCH WAS FORCED TO TAKE A DRASTIC STEP IN ORDER TO RESOLVE ITS PARKING PROBLEMS.

CHOIR SOLOIST LUANN VETZ DISCOVERS THAT HER HUSBAND ISN'T THE ONLY ONE WHO LIKES HER NEW PERFUME.

"THE BUS BROKE DOWN JUST AS THE YOUTH GROUP WAS LEAVING FOR ITS MOUNTAIN CLIMBING OUTING."

"I AM NOT CRITICIZING THE MEMBERSHIP DRIVE. ALL I'M SAYING IS THAT IT HAS CAUSED SOME NEGATIVE SIDE EFFECTS."

MANY MEMBERS OF THE CONGREGATION WERE STARTING TO THINK THAT PASTOR MILNER WAS SPREADING HERSELF TOO THIN.

THOUGH A COMPROMISE HAD BEEN MADE, THERE STILL SEEMED TO BE SOME TENSION BETWEEN PEOPLE WHO WANTED SERVICES TO BE HELD AT 9:30 A.M. AND THOSE WHO WANTED THEM AT 11:00 A.M.

"ONCE AGAIN, I WANT TO STRESS THAT THE SERMON ILLUSTRATION I'VE JUST GIVEN IS PURELY FICTIONAL AND IS NOT BASED UPON ANYONE HERE IN THE CONGREGATION."

IT WASN'T HARD TO TELL THAT THESE WERE THE FIRST VISITORS ERWIN VALLEY CHURCH HAD HAD IN SEVEN YEARS.

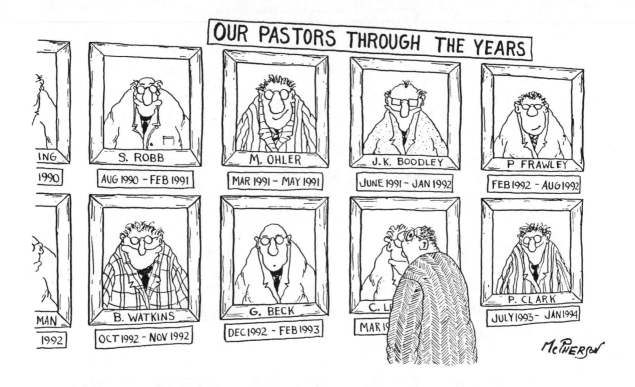

NEWLY HIRED PASTOR MILTON FELDSPAR WAS STARTING TO WONDER WHAT HE'D GOTTEN HIMSELF INTO.

"I THINK WE NEED TO START PUTTING SOME RESTRICTIONS ON THESE NON-CASH DONATIONS."

WHEN PASTORS DREAM

DUE TO HIS BUSY SCHEDULE, PASTOR ED FARNSLEY WAS FORCED TO STREAMLINE HIS BAPTISMS.

YOUTH PASTOR DAN CLYDELL FACES THE TOUGHEST SEARCH COMMITTEE OF HIS NINE-YEAR CAREER.

THE GROWTH COMMITTEE AT THE PINE CREEK CHURCH
WAS SEVERELY MISDIRECTED.

PASTOR WENDELL STAVITZ FELT IT WAS IMPORTANT TO MAKE THE CONGREGATION FEEL AT HOME.

ALTHOUGH HE HAD ONLY BEEN WITH THE CHURCH FOR ONE MONTH, PASTOR LEO ZAFNER WASTED NO TIME IN LETTING THE CHURCH BOARD KNOW WHO WAS IN CHARGE.

THE STONE VALLEY CHURCH'S SOUND SYSTEM
NEEDED SOME SERIOUS UPGRADING.

VISITORS TO PINE POINT CHURCH COULD SENSE
A CLIQUISHNESS AMONG THE CONGREGATION,
SUBTLE THOUGH IT WAS.

MᶜPHERSON

MONDAY NIGHT FOOTBALL COMMITTEE MEETING 8:30-11:30

"YEAH, I KNOW. IT'S A RIDICULOUS COMMITTEE. BUT WE WANTED TO FIND SOME WAY TO GET MORE MEN USED TO THE IDEA OF SERVING ON COMMITTEES."

TIRED OF HEARING THAT HIS SERVICES WERE BORING FOR KIDS, PASTOR LOU SELNARD GOES A LITTLE OVERBOARD.

PASTOR LUPNER DIDN'T NOTICE UNTIL HE WAS HALFWAY INTO HIS SERMON THAT HE HAD MISTAKENLY BROUGHT HIS SEVEN-YEAR-OLD'S BOOK REPORT RATHER THAN HIS SERMON.

APPARENTLY THE CHURCH'S NEW LIGHTING SYSTEM STILL HAD A FEW BUGS TO BE WORKED OUT.

OVERWHELMED BY HIS HECTIC SCHEDULE, PASTOR FARKLE BEGAN LOOKING FOR WAYS TO SAVE A FEW MINUTES HERE AND THERE.

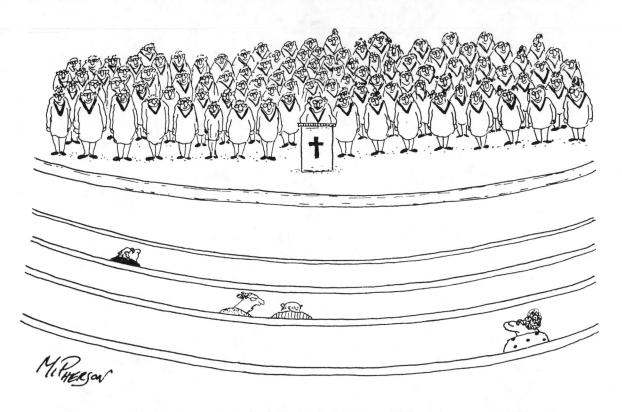

"IF YOU ASK ME, THEY GOT A LITTLE CARRIED AWAY WITH THE CHOIR MEMBERSHIP DRIVE."

YOUTH PASTOR MYRON CLANTELL WAS A MASTER
AT FINDING NEW RECRUITS.

AFTER 29 YEARS OF SERVICE, CHURCH SECRETARY MARGE FELDERN HANDS THE REINS OVER TO ELLEN FETZ.

ANOTHER CRISIS THREATENS TO DIVIDE THE CONGREGATION.

A SUNDAY SCHOOL TEACHER'S WORST NIGHTMARE: LEARNING THAT, DUE TO THE ONGOING BLIZZARD, PARENTS WON'T BE ABLE TO PICK UP THEIR KIDS FOR AT LEAST TWELVE MORE HOURS.

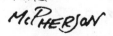

THE PASTOR'S HALL OF FAME

PMSON

NCE: 511
TEND: 264
ERMONS
TES: 51
MENT RATE:
ASKED
47
,974
HIP:

LUTHER MILMOT

- AVG. ATTENDANCE: 477
- AVG. SUN. SCH. ATTEND: 289
- CONSECUTIVE SERMONS
  WITHOUT USING NOTES: 67
- VOLUNTEER RECRUITMENT RATE:
  73% OF THOSE ASKED
- SAVES: 982
- BAPTISMS: 2,189
- AVG. CHOIR MEMBERSHIP: 49

LYLE RUGNARD

- AVG. ATTENDANCE: 493
- AVG. SUN. SCH. ATTEND: 312
- CONSECUTIVE SERMONS
  WITHOUT USING NOTES: 49
- VOLUNTEER RECRUITMENT RATE:
  82% OF THOSE ASKED
- SAVES: 1,123
- BAPTISMS: 3,043
- AVG. CHOIR MEMBERSHIP: 57

WALT SA

- AV TTEND
  SC
  N
  USIN
- VOLUNTEER R
  87% 0
  S: 1,4
  TISM
  HOI

WOW!

McPHERSON